Piece of Mine

the only word that's not spoken is a thought...express yourself

By

LaTrese D. McCullough

2010

This book of poetry is dedicated to the memories of Virginia E. McCullough, Leila McDuffy, Minnie Williams & Helen Clark.

My grandmothers who have passed on, I'm thankful for them and all of the women who helped shaped me. Grand mom Gin, you are one of the reasons I'm able to be so caring toward people today. Now I'm given the chance to share my most precious gift with the world. I love all of you and will always be proud to be your granddaughter

INTRODUCTION

A Piece of Me

As a child I would say I led a normal kid's life

Only later down the road came confusion and strife

Many years the only girl in a house wit two niggas

My pop and my brother

No sisters or a mother

Now back to my childhood, sometimes it was rough

I thank God for those times, they made me so tough

Raped, molested, at the early age of nine

Violated, disrespected, he stole what was mine

In the courtroom, on the stand, cryin' this man touched me

Stayed in the house for weeks, 'cause I felt like a dummy

Didn't take me long to really bounce back

Pulled it together, buried my feelings put it all in tact

A little later you could say moms, she went away

Left me & my brother alone and astray

We was cool we had Aunt Deb, grandmoms and dad

Even though she wasn't there, things weren't so bad

Time flew, got older, had Tay, my 1st seed

Graduated school, got a job & smoked a lil' weed

A new era, 2000 had Asiah, my baby girl

As she took her first breath, her twin didn't make it in the world

Stressful, traumatic, I lost my child so dear

Couldn't cope or get over it, I was depressed for a year

In and outta dumb stuff by the age of 21

Couldn't see it then, just thought I was havin' fun

Now back to the story of all the trauma and grief

Been thru so much drama beyond recognition & belief

The thing that hurt the most, when I lost my Grandmom Gin

She was the best, not just a grandmom but also a friend

A hard time for my family but we was there for each other

My dad was so hurt he lost his dear mother

Keepin it movin, got locked up, did a bid, why me?

Who would've guessed that would've happened in 2003

Prison, believe me its worse than they say

All I did was laugh, play cards & eat chi-chi's all day

Like they say what don't kill you, makes you even stronger

Glad I got out when I did, I couldn't take jail much longer

But I used that time to get focused and calm down

Cause' the road was gonna' be different next time around

Leading up to 2004, an ok year of my life

Things a lil easier, gettin better, a lil less strife

Yet another tragic event, my nigga Capone pronounced dead

They took him out this world wit a bullet to the head

I loved him to death, I wear his name on my chest

On November the 8th he was laid to final rest

My days still going steady I have my ups and my downs

Hide my pain by turned around frowns

The years flying by, 2005 came and went

Done been thru it all with or without a red cent

Let's see, got my own crib, a few gigs

Still setbacks here and there

But nothing so hard, that God knew I couldn't bear

My days going by, the clock tickin' steady

I know that there's better, just gotta be ready

Feels like time just started, but great thus far

And at the age of 26, I've came so far

But each step I take, I keep fallin' back

Times get even harder when I'm on the right track

Now on foreign ground, to start over and blend in

But can't seem to get past that one unveiling sin

I feel used and abused, still searching for my task

Tryna gain comfort and strength to take off my mask

Tryna be a good girl, getaway and hide out

And 2007 was when it all came about

With the world steady turnin, movin up each degree

I'm pourin' out my soul, giving you a piece of me

Reflection

In the mirror, I see a reflection

But am I aware of who I see?

Is it light fragments touching glass, or is it really me?

I'm afraid to step out to see

What lies beneath

But the pain that I'm enduring I cannot keep

Bottled emotions lead to mental distraught

I try to run from my feelings but damn I'm caught

Caught in a cyclone of ups and downs

I conceal my pain wit upside down frowns

On the interior my heart is burning

And on the other end my soul is yearning

Yearning for the answer to my question

When will I truly know my reflection?

By: Lauren Williams

"Yes, I need to get myself together
'cause I got someplace to go"

TABLE OF CONTENTS

Chapter One-<u>Me Time. A Moment of Expression</u>...

Chapter Introduction

On My Way

Chapter Two-Jail Time. Soul searching, trying to grow up…

Chapter Introduction

11

Chapter 3-<u>A Time of Love & Happiness. Is it all that it's</u>
<u>cracked up to be?</u>

Chapter Introduction

Family

CHAPTER 1
Me Time. A moment of expression

I spent years wasting time, trying to "find out what I wanted to be when I grow up." The problem with that was I was already grown. I was always trying to be something that I wasn't. I would sit and think and fathom ideas of how I was going to get rich, but I didn't even have a plan. I have so many great ideas, but that's just it, they're only ideas, nothing but great ideas. Just potential, and no real progress. But the truth was, I didn't have a clue about any of those ideas, they were just as nonexistent as my life at that point.

God has really shown me to use the gifts that he has given me and the situations I've been thru to grow from them and educate people. I've had to overcome so many hindrances and barriers in my time, sometimes I feel older than what I really am. I've been thru molestation, abusive relationships, teenage pregnancy, jail, joblessness, being broke, busted and disgusted, and even in the worst of situations, my voice still present. I feel there's no way I shouldn't be able to handle what comes my way. If we all just gave up or get depressed with the many life situations we encounter, nothing would ever be worth it. I had to learn to fully embrace who I was and use it to my advantage. I am a unique designer's original; there is no other LaTrese Denise McCullough in this world, who is supposed to walk the path I'm walking. *No one is better at being me then me!* "Rise up above all that people say, and out of those things that you think you'll never get over and do great things with yourself, you are you're biggest investment."

On My Way

Walk out the door

The wind hits my cheeks

Frozen to a point, they red as beets

Brisk, chilly, below zero outside

Get on my little hike, in desperate need of a ride

Coldest morning yet, exceeding the others by far

Need to get warm, should have a drink at the bar

Better grab a coffee to go

Damn! There goes the bus passing by Oh no!

Gonna' be late that's my pattern, gotta go

Better get movin', 'cause I need that dough

The sun shining bright the wind blowing strong

Can see it already this day is gonna' be long

What a perfect start to this morning, Sike!

By the time I get to work I'll be an icicle from this hike

Badlands

It's funny how life goes

What'll happen next, no one knows

Gangstas live then they die

Thugs hug the block, blow tree & get high

The Ricans I know, Latin Kings and Queens

Don't have a care in the world, will kill you by any means

All types of people grow up in the hood

A handful of bad and a couple of good

Seen too much, too quick, throughout this life

Half was positive, the rest caused strife

Most of my homies went to jail or hell

What'll happen to me, only time will tell

My kids are all I live for

And I promised them I won't leave them no more

Help a Sistah Out

Is she focused or just frontin'

Take a deep breath cause she don't know what she want, and

Every man she meets is just a regular Joe

And the females she hang wit make her look like a hoe

And on Sunday it's church music and all praises to God

On the flip side it's getting drunk and showin' her behind

In her mind it's not wrong to sin and go to church

But it's that worldly mentality that keeps her at her worst

Now somebody, are you listening, JUST HELP THIS SISTAH OUT!

Cause what's goin' thru her mind is confusion and self doubt

While some struggle with depression or even abuse

And other women it's fornication and a lil' drug use

I don't mean to step on ya toes or hurt the way you feel

But at this point in my life, I just gotta' keep it real

Lemme' break it down, I got a story to tell

It was at this point in my life when I chose heaven over hell

Facing the wrong way

One foot in and one foot out

Something touched deep inside, began to cry, start to shout

Knelt down by the altar feeling blue, feeling low

Heard a lil' voice saying "just take it and go"

My walk, brighter less time to pout

Somebody please, will you HELP THIS SISTAH OUT

Mirror

I stare in the mirror day after day

Try to figure out why I act this way

It must be something deep inside of me

Hidden like a treasure lost at sea

The look in my eyes, so empty, so lost

My life; like a movie but at what cost?

Those times I thought it would be all good

Must've been high, and so misunderstood

That fast life costs you, but the question is what?

Could lose your being or be in self disrupt

These feelings, trust me they're real

Sat behind bars wondering what was the deal

Everybody makes mistakes, don't get me wrong

Best believe what don't kill you, will only make you strong

21

Where am I?

Stuck in the same place and nowhere to go

Trying to elevate and can't even grow

No money or wealth to brag on or show

This can't be my path say it ain't so

Hoping one day soon, a lifetime of riches

Feeling a lil' left back, down in the dumps & ditches

I'm destined to become some prosperous girl

Create my own unstoppable world

With no questions, still I'll remain true

To all that I love and all that I do

Try to take good care of my kids

Transformed, I just did it

Family comes first; they hold the key to my heart

Without them I wouldn't know where to start

I'm gonna' make the most out of my life time

Was born to be great, would say she's a dime

Many would say a diamond in the rough

And I always want more, don't seem to have enough

Overly confident, not extreme as cocky

A little thick in the waist but I wouldn't say stocky

A beautiful girl both inside and out

Gonna' reach my full potential without a shadow of a doubt

Back to reality, still stuck in this place

But I will come in first at the end of my race

One Standpoint

Gotta' move, Gotta' run, Gotta' get out of here

It's like ya feet stuck in cement, showing nothing but fear

Be quick, be strong, be on point, and be alert

In the long run don't want ya feelings to be hurt

Stand up, stand proud, stand and don't sit

Go for what you know: keep ya head up, that's it

Stay focused, stay ahead, and be able to adjust

Go wit ya first instinct, do what you must

Move forward, move about, move around, and move in

Cant's stay idle too long, be gone in the wind

In & out, up & down, never side to side

At some point learn how to swallow ya pride

Show emotion, show concern, show ya strength to prevail

Keep ya eyes on the prize, don't let ya train derail

Remain calm, remain easy, remain the same always

Keep in mind, here on earth, numbered are your days

Speak slowly, speak humbly, and speak when spoken to

Watch your surroundings, watch what you say and do

Not good to just browse or stay in one spot

Keep in mind that's how some people get got!

Once you're involved it's hard to let go and get out

Especially once you got pull and have a little clout

You'll lose some; you'll win some, but ultimately try

And there will come a time when you have to say
Goodbye...

Ideas

Living in a world that's so unreal

No one who understands, to tell how I feel

Humanity itself is always so cold

To survive one must be and remain so bold

Situations arise both to and fro

There are some things in time that must be let go

For instance: money makes the world go round

More money more problems, many have found

In order to love others you must first love yourself

We often love for wrong reasons, one being wealth

Opportunity won't always come knockin' at your door

Don't settle for less, always go after more

You won't always be walkin' down easy street

And one wrong turn doesn't mean defeat

The road to success is not paved in gold

And wisdom will come as one grows old

Adamantly seek both knowledge and truth

In a prosperous world we must educate our youth

Knock and doors will open, seek and you shall find

Passing judgment on others requires a clear and sound mind

What goes around always comes back to you

That's how karma works, so watch what you do

When in doubt, go with the feeling deep in your gut

It will steer you right without an if, and, or but

These things will prove true throughout your life span

And don't go thru time guessing have a well thought out plan

Past, Present and Future

A lil' struggle, a lil' pain, what can I say that's life

Some triumph, some tragedy, cut deeper than any knife

Mistakes, misfortunes, delusions of the mind

Mysterious to others, unique, one of a kind

Some things to be forgotten, set aside, buried within

Replay all the memories in my head time and time again

My childhood experience made me grow up too fast

As I glance at the future and reflect on the past

A woman, a mother, this present day in age

A lil' torn, a lil' stronger, body filled wit' rage

My cup overflowing with secrets from my soul

Still searching for that someone whom with I can grow old

Always looking for a true friend who won't judge me in spite of

And I don't know if and when I'll ever find true love

My mind steady racin', too many thoughts fill my head

This life I lead, like a novel waitin' to be read

In my twenties, but feels like I been here fifty years

Because of all that I been thru, from those many tears

Hasn't been all bad, there was laughter here and there

At one moment I gave up, nowadays I'm starting to care

My angels, here on earth, keep me calm and cool

Never trust anyone, that's my #1 rule

My true essence blossoming, my attitude getting better

I figured out that life isn't all about ya cheddar

Used to think the earth revolved around me

Took many nights in jail for me to actually see

What life is all about

The bigger picture to make out

Striving to be a role model, someone to look up to

To give advice to my children, "you can only be you"

To live wonderful and lavish

Equipped with understanding and compassion

One day reach the golden years and reminisce thru out
time

And wonder at one point why I chose to commit crime

Later down the road I'll reflect and look back

And remember when I got my life on the right track

Tryna' figure out what's next is hard to say

Just live to your fullest each and every day

What my future holds is always in arms reach

And I figured out my purpose in life is to teach

As I grow older gaining knowledge and wisdom

Prepare myself for all the discoveries to come

Discoveries

To reach my full potential, will it happen here on earth?

With all this self confidence, do I have self worth?

Covering on the outside, what lies deep within

Stir up confusion enough to make my head spin

Soul searching tryna' find this person called LaTrese

Trapped emotions but no courage to escape or release

Rising high above the clouds like a jet thru the sky

Can't come up with an answer, just the question Why?

At the end of my rainbow will there be a pot of gold

Will I die at a young age or will I grow to be old

It's the past that shapes the future

But the future reflects the past

And the present days we live in, tell the tales of the last

Why Me?

Today, today only I've had it up to here

I'm tryna' think straight but my mind ain't even clear

What's wrong, I'm gonna' snap, feel like I wanna' fight

If somebody rubs me wrong, I don't know, I just might

I need to be quiet, be peaceful, and relax

Just keep still like candle wax

Adrenaline rising, I need to fall back and pray

This job, these kids, so many issues

Complex, stressful, but what's a girl to do

My path is so foggy, I can't even see

Lift my hands to the sky and ask Why me?

Tricks

It's like I have nothing to say if it ain't about pain

I feel so confident to the point that I'm vain

Sometimes my walk is hard and I let myself down

Put a mask on everyday to cover up this frown

I've realized the one thing that keeps holding me back

It's myself that won't let me stay on the right track

I'm so bad it's like I don't wanna' be me

And my kids, the only ones who will actually see

The nights when I'm all alone, and can't stop crying

The laughs and jokes I share but inside really dying

I'll go hard for awhile than back to being lazy

My life is like a riddle, am I smart or just crazy

Why I keep dealing wit' men, and getting nothing in return

I'm gonna' find myself in hell where my soul eternally burns

Nah! That's not the path set out for me

It's just the enemy playing one of his many tricks on me

This Tale

Irreconcilable difference

A broken trust

Thinkin' real hard, gonna' take a ride on a bus

No place to go, no destination in mind

Sit back & dream, watch time rewind

Once upon a time! The story will start

No happy ending just a broken heart

Somewhere beyond there lies our bond

Could rise even stronger with the wave of a wand

And magically we could have that fairy tale ending

And make amends of this time apart we're spending

One sweet day we'll live happily ever after

Our eyes filled wit' tears, souls bubbling wit' laughter

Reassurance

I need reassurance.

Distressed, distraught, confusion set in

Facin' a brick wall, unsure of where to begin

Emotions ragin' as water in the sea

A decision to make and it's not easy

Outcome so precious

Equally so wrong

A roller coaster of emotions

But knew what to do all along

Life Is

What's really goin' on? Is this a dream or is it real

Will somebody please tell me what's the deal?

I need an ounce of strength just to go on

Been in & out of struggle since the day I was born

Life can be misleading confusing at times

Many of us driven to a life of crime

Life can be a puzzle, pieces scattered everywhere

People don't know whether to go here or there

Life can also be simple and plain

So transparent like a drop of rain

Life can be a picture in your favorite book

Or a good song but without the hook

Life can be complex, even complicated

In order to succeed one must be educated

Life can be beautiful as a perfect red rose

But what'll happen next no one ever knows

Think about this, life can be all that you make it

Just grab it by the hand and take it

In life be sure to be all you can be

Remember in life, nothing is free

The 113

Why you so chunky, and sit next to me

My body so squished I can hardly breathe

Damn! I shouldda' kept that bag in the seat

Cause you squeezing my knees and all of my meat

Now you know you can't fit all of that in the seat

So move over a lil' cause you drawin' too much heat

It's cool for a minute just get up real soon

And give me some space and some breathing room

You big but I'm glad that you don't have a stink

But the longer you sit, the more I sink

What a relief, your stop is up next

Cause I was starting to get mad, a lil' heated and vexed

But what about the rest of the broads on the bus

Looking at them with total awe & disgust

A fitted hat, a tied up shirt on top of some weave

A faux fox wrapped around her neck and her sleeve

Giant bumps protruding from her face and her neck

Another busted Reeboks, lookin' like a train wreck

A little ruffled, but can't stop it's makin' me sick

Why did I have to take this 113 trip?

Poetic Sagittarius

Poetic passion, so lyrical

God's gift to me, a wonderful lil' miracle

Try to compare me to who?

Verses flaming fire, bright light shining thru

Motivational rhymes

Inspired by tryin' times

Soulful energy expressed

Overloaded, emotionally stressed

A slight sense of pain

Poems like venom; insane

Spiritual, full of romance

Words graceful; song & dance

An archer in company of a bow and arrow

Embodied with a radiant glow

Outside

Costume jewelry is all she wears

You will always see weave instead of her hair

If you don't love yourself who will ever love you

Always stay fly, that's what she do

Looks like a million bucks, whenever she come thru

Her face never filled with make-up though

Victoria secret lip gloss, Mac eye shadow

Calvin Klein keeps her smelling good

Her wardrobe a combo between relaxed and hood

Stiletto's maybe, but she's so laid back

Keep everything plain, simple, that's that

Her basis clean, appearance of sexy

Not too hard for her, it comes naturally

Exclusive and stylish individual

Her swagger, her lingo, just so original

From head to toe and down to the "T"

But that's only the outside you see

Everyday

Faced wit' a reality not easy to accept

Her biggest problems seem minor to the rest

Tryna' stays focused, and stay on the grind

Too much stress building up on her mind

Attention directed to her beautiful daughters

Cause she gotta' take care of 'em come hell or high waters

Making excuses, the feeling of lame

Tryna' live up to this person, this name

Wearing too many hats, working too many jobs

Indiscretion on the low as if she were in the mob

This is every day, not just one, but many

She often feels like her being is almost insanity.

This Chick

When she was in school

Dreams about going to college

Getting a good job, gain powerful knowledge

But plans often change

Things went down a different way

She started slippin' up in school

Attracting all the wrong men

Turned out and lost by the age of 16

Getting' in trouble, actin' crazy

In high school dealin' green

Her boyfriend (so she called him) an old head, & her peoples ain't like 'em

Dey baby girl knocked up

Dey all wanted to fight 'em

It started wit' cookin' his stash up & keepin' his guns

A full time wifey, no time for teenage fun

She was all in love and didn't know what it meant

Waitin' at home for dis nigga and he would come home bent

She even lived wit' him now

In a house wit' his moms

And at the age of 28 he even went on her prom

He went from this dude that liked her,

To a baby girl being born

She was a lil' girl, now a grown woman scorn

Trust, this nigga was crazy

Matter fact he still is

Dats' why he behind bars and

Won't be home for some years

But back to the old days, gotta' story to tell

Because of shit dat' she did, that's why she going to hell

Remember the time her man got booked

Murder 1 was the charge, she was shaken and shook

She couldn't take it no more

An alcoholic, daily

And everything was a party

And funny thing was

She committed them charges…

Pay the Toll

Sometimes I take shit for what it's worth

Or I'll question myself, whichever thought comes first

Knee deep in confusion; caught up with expression

Only one step away from a stage of depression

Gather my thoughts with a pad and a pen

A delusion of my mind, this notebook my best friend

Crazy, erratic, a psychopathic individual

Far past gone, slightly residual

5 feet 9 inches drowning from the rain

Resistant to life's beat downs, like numbness of cocaine

Sadly mistaken, so very misunderstood

Condemned like abandoned buildings that lie in the hood

Torn, raggedy edges make a beautiful finish

And 5 times out of 10 they crumble and diminish

Equip for the game and ready for battle

Calm and serene like a baby and rattle

This world turned into a chaotic mess

Can't be weak minded, or be too stressed

All around the globe, among each and every soul

Awaits an answer to the question who will pay the toll

It's Like

It's like everything's a disappointment, one great big let down

Facin' a bigger brick wall every time I turn around

It's like I can't get no help, nobody has my back

I keep struggling to do my best and stay on the right track

It's like things are getting harder & my money getting tight

And every time I turn around I'm ready to snap or ready to fight

It's like the people I wanna' trust just keep letting me down

And I wanna' keep smilin' but it's too easy to frown

It's like I'm happy on the outside but hurtin' deep within

And I can't share my feelings wit no one, just kept within

It's like I try hard to portray like things are under control

But I keep getting snake eyes when I pick up the dice and roll

It's like I keep landin' on bankrupt in this life of wheel of fortune

And I try to keep a steady pace but I'm always on the run

It's like I'm tryna' rid my weakness & let my strength take over

And it's hard to kick bad habits, like going thru life being sober

It's like no matter what people say I still feel I'm a good person

But what shows first is all the bad I've done

It's like I want so much outta' life but can't get past the start

And I wanna' fall in love and be married, but don't want a broken heart

It's like I know I'm a good mother, I love my daughters to no end

And I try hard to compromise but it's just so hard to bend

It's like I try to make good choices and try to right my wrongs

And I can't express my feelings wit out a poem or a song

It's like I take ten steps forward then go back three spaces

It's like this & like that, if it ain't one thing it's another

So Tired

Tired of rhyming about niggas, tired of verses dealin' wit pain

I need a happy thought to arise something good to come outta' me

Like layin on a white sand beach, next to sparkling blue waters

Or a hot summer day in the park wit' my daughters

This hectic life I lead, sometimes hard to find peace

But then again if I were perfect, then who would be LaTrese

This day in age, things are crazy, life ain't fun no more

Potential to be a victim each time you walk out ya door

Everybody got a gun, murders left and right

Something tragic fills the news each & every night

Nowadays things are critical, generation Y gone wild

Every action is over the edge, nothing simple, nothing mild

51

But as the world evolves humanity forced to change its ways

But as the revelations states we livin' in the last days

What happened to those happy thoughts & sweet pleasant dreams?

Instead we have reality & nightmares; so it seems

Life is getting worse and going down the drain

My daughters keep me focused, keep me from being insane

If I had no kids, I would be really out of control

Doing shit wit out a conscience & wouldn't care about a soul

On a mission out for self, committed to prosperity and gaining.

Growing so much and maturing, my kids taught me a lot

Beginning to see the big picture and make out the plot

So tired of writing about tragedy and the sadness I feel

But I can't lie or front, just gotta' keep it real.

Sleep on That

It's like I was born to be bad, but try so hard to do good

Livin' life in the suburbs, yet so ghetto, so hood

Life is supposed to be good, but so much pain do I encounter

And I try to make it better wit' smiles and wit laughter

Disappearing acts being pulled and I don't trust no man

And there's always that one person tryna' mess up my life's plan

When I needed my friends the most, they wasn't there, turned their backs

And I'm tellin' ya'll its hard, watching ya mom strung out on crack

Trying times I can remember being pregnant in high school

Or being behind bars being punished and, treated cruel

Struggling wit' my kids tryna do it all alone

Cut my childhood short, forced to mature and be grown

At one point I thought times wouldn't ever get no better

Cause I been thru those days wit' no job or no cheddar

Being hit, beaten up, abused by my man

Never thought I'd see the day when he would raise his hand

Those experiences, situations taught me a very important lesson

Really they weren't curses, turned out to be blessings

I'm living proof, life does always progress

And those rough patches I went thru turned out to be a test

My tears now filed wit' joy my smiles more sincere

My life reaching higher plains year after year

Things that used to get me down I don't let 'em get me stressed

And God is the only reason why I'm being so blessed

My parents, I thank them dearly, taught me how to survive

Helped me make it in this world showed me to fight and strive

Like they say the apple don't fall too far from the tree

And nobody can ever say that it was easy being me

I walked a hard walk took me awhile to reach this point

And I got my daughters to raise up, can't let 'em down or disappoint

My life has been filled wit' good times along wit' trouble and pain

And everything I once lost God has helped me to regain

And to all the females struggling sittin' in the same seat I once sat

I love ya'll, be strong, it gets better, Sleep on that

What's Next

If I treat it like silver

Then I guess gold comes next

Tryna be this great person

At least live my best

But you know "Trese ain't gone change

That's what they all say

And my pop and my brother dey' gonna' continue to pray

My moms, she keep it real cause she been thru a struggle

Watched me ova the years, in and out of trouble

Now I'm tryna raise my kids to the best of capability

Gotta' be a good mom, Tay & Asiah look up to me

I been in and out of relationships, some good and some bad

Just reflectin' back on the memories that I have

My grand mom, she gone away but I wish she was here

I wear her ring on my finger just to keep her near

My family, I love 'em greatly but we strangers sometimes

Cause my feelings always secret you only hear 'em in my rhymes

But as for me, what's next? Cause I had enough struggle

Done been in enough trouble

Just need to praise God, I love 'em

Cause he brought me outta' this and he delivered me from that

And when I went astray put me on the right track

I'm tellin' ya'll if he can save me

LaTrese Denise McCullough

Then he can save you, ya father, sister and ya mother

Now, what's next I ask again? Cause I'm tired of all this rain

Can't take no more pain

I'm ready for a change

I need to "Get myself together 'cause I got someplace to go"

Can't hang my head low, can't be depressed no mo'

'Cause I ain't go thru all this pain just to end up the same

And my story gone be heard my breath thru spoken word

So no matter what you been thru, what you seen or what you heard

He'll make it all better, he promised in his word

Me or She

It just ain't that easy you see

Used to ask the question Why me?

Why life is twice as hard for me

Why couldn't somebody else be me?

What does the future hold for me?

She needs a looking glass to see

As a matter of fact it's all about me, me, me

This wanna be diva you see

A cute face, all in the right place

Yeah! That be she

Intellectually, sensually, selfishly

Honestly described to a "T"

Nonchalantly she tries to be

Chicks practice to act like she

I take pride in being me

Broken and cold heartedly

Transformation and change a part of me

Distantly facin' reality

Each moment a new challenge for me

Capítol La-Tr-ese, that's me

So who is she?

A black girl lost, rebellious without a cause

That used to be she

Enlightened wit individuality

Cursed by heredity

Looking thru her reflection for a better image of she

A few old ways, a few new make up the present she

That gangsta she, a part of past me

Holding on tryna embrace this new path for me

Cause tomorrow brings about a change in she

So believe half of what you hear and some of what you see

Cause half of what you get is some of she

The other half some of me.

Puzzles

Sometimes I sell myself short,

You know like a paragraph when it should be a book report

Drive my focus where it shouldn't be

Knowing the situation won't grow to be

Happily ever after, more like an emotional disaster

Daily visits to a factory

Not exactly the way it's supposed to be

I'll take a henny and some wings

Mixed wit' all the worries life brings

Blackened lungs on cloud nine

Waiting on a nigga to wine and dine

Two seeds comin' up too fast

Not enough time or enough cash

But they say life is what you make it

So is it better if you just fake it

And who is "they"

I guess it's just something people say

And since life is like a puzzle

And everyone a key piece

I gotta' find a spot for this girl named LaTrese

CHAPTER 2

Jail Time.
Soul searching, trying to grow up

We live in a world too close for comfort. When we should stick together the most, we spread ourselves apart. Sometimes I sit back and think how I can trust others when I don't even trust myself. I make my world so complicated by these same choices I keep making. It almost becomes a pattern or a bad habit, and you know what they say "Old habits die slow". My life could be twice as easy as but instead I have to work at it twice as hard. I'm tired of chalking everything up to experience, or being taught one of life's many lessons. I need my big break, I need to hit my lick and keep on moving. I don't want to end up with nothing by the time my kids are grown, and that's right around the corner. So what's a young woman like me doing knee deep in her own ball of confusion, which is actually my life. A friend of mine told me he liked me because I'm so down to earth. Or is that the earth has put me down? I'm too smart to be in dumb shit, too intelligent to just be here in this world and not make something of myself. No really I am! So just wait, hold on, because my train just pulled up and I gotta' get on it, 'cause it might be the last one pulling out the station and I can't miss it.

That's exactly what my life feels like sometimes, a train ride. A little bumpy, sometimes noisy, a little cramped for my style, sometimes stop & go, and sometimes it's a smooth ride. But anyway let me tell it, and "Everything's gonna' be alright," but you can judge that for yourself.

True Feelings

Did I throw my life away?

Ahead must be a better day

Closer to the end of times

Look around see the signs

Things ain't the same no more

To some jail has a revolving door

It's such a miserable place

Your life just goes to waste

You feel cripple and can't walk

Speechless, can't talk

Treated so bad, lower than dirt

Heart holding nothing but hurt

Your back against the wall

Not even a space to crawl

A dark cloud hanging over your head

Feel like the walking dead

Maybe a sitting duck

With nothing but bad luck

Raining so hard on your life

Time after time discord and contention

Couldn't possible get any worse

Is this a bad dream or a curse?

Is there a limit to this madness?

In the end left with loneliness and sadness

Sitting

Sitting here stressing and all alone

Can't get out not even to go home

Try to hold on try to be strong

Keep telling myself "Trese, it won't be long"

My girls need me and I need my freedom

When will my day ever come?

All my fault only me to blame

Turned myself in, should've never came!

Soon it'll be over I can feel it deep inside

Nothing left to lose not even my pride

Am I gonna see a rainbow when the downpour clears

Who will wait on me and wipe away my tears

Please, Not Today

Don't tell me one thing and then do another

Just keep it real or don't even bother

I'm so disappointed 'cause I didn't see Taijah

And so deeply hurt not to visit with Asiah

No one to be mad at other than me

So easy to put blame on anyone you see

Who would have ever thought, Trese would be sitting in jail

A flight risk they say, holding me wit no bail

Reading the bible, day in and day out

Hoping and praying that scripture brings me out

Out of this mess of my so called life

I always ask the question, Why me? Why me? For what reason I say, the answer is visible to see

Trouble is easy to get into, but hard as hell to get out of

I wouldn't wish prison on anyone I love

Maybe a few enemies could use a life sentence

Now I'm in repentance

My words come to an end on this last and final note

Please, not today, I might choke slam you by the throat

So What...

So what I'm locked up, and you can throw away the key

I have not a soul to fault other than me

This cold ass jail, this nasty ass food

I'm really, really not in the mood

But like I said, So what!

There goes that bad attitude back in effect. Cause everything ain't going my way

I wanna be mad, so mad, but why

There's really no reason not even to cry

It's enough that I'm here in this county prison

Can't see my daughters who I'm deeply missin

Hard enough that life is just passin me by

But a bitch is too strong and I refuse to cry

For what, there's no purpose, don't see one at all

Right now life's one big ass downfall

But like I said, So what!

That's how it is sometimes, So what!

Renee

Renee, Renee, you love to play. You didn't have to throw
that juice my way

I was only joking, of course you spit when you talk

Take the joke to the chin, turn around and walk

It probably wasn't right that I pulled your hair

But you have to admit, it was only fair

It's over, done with just put it to an end

'Cause when it's all said and done, you will never win

To argue and fight it's not worth it at all

But if it has to come to that point, I never turn down a
brawl

You claim to be holy, an evangelist you say

But why did you ever throw that juice my way

73

Change for Two

Tell me what it is that makes me feel this way

My attitude must be changing I've just been writing away

Instead of picking a fight, I'll just send someone a kite

Ask my celly, she'll tell you all I do is write

She reads and I write then laugh and talk all night

Two grown women in this cell, and we both lil silly

My background lies in Philly and she from Atlantic City

Of course we'll keep in touch from this day to the next

But when we're released, who knows what'll happen next

Miss C/O

Just cause you work in a prison, doesn't give you all the power

So what we wanna change the T.V. every other hour

Its bad enough we locked up, in jail, Oh my God!

With no place to go other than this pod

I may be in jail but at least I ain't ugly

This is only temporary, what can you say honey.

I can't concentrate even to write these verses

So hard to write without using curses

I can't wait to get out and I ain't ever comin back!

I've laughed and played enough, I wish it was over

I can't take this no more, especially being sober

Now I know what you're thinking, I'm not on drugs or a drunk

And don't ever mistake me for being a punk

75

This started out as simple poetry for the C/O

But turned into reality, can't you see, don't you know!

Let me end this lil poem, I better before I cry

Sike! I'm only kidding, but that's the end, Goodbye

Jokes

If I'm keeping you up late at night

Don't talk behind my back, let's just fight

Oh I forgot ya'll some bitches

Maybe even a few snitches

We just be laughin', havin' fun

Cause in a few days it'll all be done

My girl is leavin', returnin' to her home

As for me I'll be all alone

But that's alright there will be another soon

Then the jokes start all over beginning from noon

We played trouble all night, at least 'til 2

It's so boring in here we had nothing to do

Don't hate 'cause ya'll tryna sleep

In a few days you won't hear a peep

San is leavin', going home, for real, Word is Bond!

Leavin' me here with these nuts far past gone

Oh my God, I gotta' stop this, it's really such a bore

Ya'll just lucky we ain't keep you up 'til 4

A Thought

The sun shining so bright

Lying in this cell, with my thoughts that I write

So tired of writing, and being locked in

This yellow paper, this commissary pen

My mind steady racing, my heart beat as well

Sweat pouring down my face as if I'm living in hell

At the end of the tunnel there may be a ray

All I can do is hope and pray

My race cut too short, I have not yet fought

Left sitting in this place with just a mere thought

No Place

A jail is not the place for me

So much better than this that's easy to see

Sick and tired of writing prison verses

Poems filled with anger and curses

This cell, this bunk, the women on this pod

Thursday night church, praying to God

Can't even sleep, no appetite to eat

Prison life, so tired and beat

Vents blowing nothing but cold air

Tired of wearing these braids in my hair

I need to go home, just let me be

A jail is not the place for me

Friday Night

An end to a long, stressful day

Down on bending knees to pray

Up at sunrise then back to sleep

A great deal of time to sit and weep

2nd grade games trouble, scrabble and others

One movie a week, what kinda' life is that

Locked in a cell for half the day

Commissary each week don't give it away

Visits on three days of the week

Looking forward to that kiss placed upon my cheek

Writing rhymes lying on the bottom bunk

Its Friday night and I wish I were drunk

Evening

All alone and so cold

Locked up, drugs being sold

Feeling empty and distressed

One of God's many tests

Blasting the radio, nowhere to go

Counting the days, to go before a judge

In suspense, cause she might hold a grudge

Encouraging words from a close friend

Letters and poems he'll send

More and more I wanna' cry

But this time too shall pass by

No Where

Gonna' live in good existence

Without so much friction

Gotta' be there for my kids

Can't do no more jail bids

Cause there is no crime

Not backed up by time

Gotta' give up too much, costs too much

Feeling paralyzed and handicap

Can't do nothing but fall back

Try to figure out where you went wrong

Ain't seen the streets in so long

Nowhere to go, nothing to do

Lost and totally blue

Cherish the moments you had

Old pictures lined up on the wall

Separated from family, can't even call

No sex, no cable, no smoke

Food so nasty I choke

This is the worst place ever

I won't come back here never!

Birthday

My birthday weekend another year gone by

Will I live to see tomorrow?

Wondering, pondering anticipating my release

My number at the top of the list awaiting my turn

Judgment day is coming soon

Been waiting patiently, Oh so long

Gather all my thoughts together

Prayed up, well rested, shielded by the word

My number shall soon be called

Quit It

Just another ordinary day

Nothing's changed, what can I say

My neck aches, its cold in here

Calling out to God, for my mind to be clear

Feeling serene, feeling calm

As a psychic reading a palm

Nonsense that I'm writing down

Emotions lame, kinda' feel like a clown

Lord, please help me write a good rhyme

Put my pen down, try another time

Months

Spent all of November behind bars, locked in

Away from my girls and all of my kin

Remain so humble and meek

Stay in the word, saw myself getting weak

Proud of myself, I really have grown

Throughout this struggle, thru time I have learned

A great deal of purpose, for it was written

Great deals of discord, my turn to be smitten

Like the army, BE ALL YOU CAN BE

Make the best of a your catastrophe

Worst comes to worst, fall on bending knee to pray

Trust in God, he'll lead the way

Time

All this time to meditate and reflect, why not take the time
to find yourself

May get to something hidden deep inside

May be respectable, may be shocking, it may build your
pride

Prison can always be an experience

Time away to become a worthy soul

Build your character, it makes you strong

Crying doesn't make it any better

When all the tears run down your cheek

Still enclosed

Still trapped

The strong survive, the weak will crumble

Do your time, don't let it do you

Unless it lasts forever, the storm will soon clear

After you've climbed to the top of the mountain, purpose you'll realize

Look back at the struggle

Was it all worth it?

No where left to go but forward

Trapped

It's raining, it's pouring

My celly, still snoring

So cold, so damp

My legs all cramped

Hungry, starving

Starvin' like Marvin

So tired, so sick

Sick of this shit

I'm trippin', I'm snappin'

Why did this have to happen?

Will I ever go home, will I ever get out

My kids need me now, for real, no doubt

Lost, trapped an emotional wreck

Holding it together, keepin' it in check

"Can't take it no more" reachin' out to God

These officers, this cell, being stuck on this pod

Never had to sit still this long

When I get out this time, ain't doin' no more wrong!

A Lil' Better

Another night passed

Time standing still, this can't last

Poems-like chicken soup for my soul

Each verse-like another filling bowl

Behind these walls in each & every cell

Awaits a testimony for each woman to tell

A change took place deep in my heart

Knowing that God gave me a new start

Wanna' change, the whole world to know

From here on 'til the very day I go

See Me Thru

Lord what shall I do?

I have to face this situation

Lead the way

I know you will see me thru

My enemies have gathered together

Tell me what to do now

My heart filled with hurt, stomach churning

Trembling & shaking, scared to come face to face

I know it's not easy

But I have faith you'll See Me Thru

Her

Take the time to get to know me

Though you may like what you see

Don't judge this lady from the outside

What counts is hidden deep inside

A little proud, a little funny

Loves to shop, loves money

A real friend when it's all said and done

Loves to party loves to have fun

A good mother, sister, daughter and niece

I'm talking about her, not LaTrese!

CHAPTER 3

A Time of Happiness & Love...
Is it all that it's cracked up to be?

Happiness huh, is it highly overrated? Maybe, the answer to my problems. Is all this just an illusion or mirage, something we all crave but may never attain? And if we are ever to find the love or happiness that we often crave, will it actually be all that we expected or anticipated? Or will it be contentment. Can you ever be truly happy or totally in love? Why do we live our lives in the pursuit of happiness? Because once you reach that point will it be enough or will you always want more. More money, more peace, more of the things and people that we love the most. That would only mean that we are achieving different levels of happiness, not complete happiness, but happiness in certain aspects of our lives, but not all. If we are successful career wise but have an average social life, is that enough to be happy? Or could you be madly in love and like your minimum wage job and achieve the same feeling. For real, what makes me happy can make another person sad. And what does being "happy" actually mean? Is it when you wake up with a smile on your face 'cause you just think life is so great, or is it that tear that rolls down your cheek when you're crying tears of joy? Women often deal with emotion, so at times they might base their happiness hastily on affairs of the heart. Men often deal with ego and machismo. And what fuels that is most often a form of happiness for men. But ultimately the pursuit of each one's happiness is individual and personal. So the answer to the initial statement "Is happiness highly overrated," No it is only over anticipated, and underappreciated. But deep down inside "Are you really happy with yourself?" Because you can't love anyone else or ever be happy with anyone until you are with yourself.

"You have to be your own best friend before you can be a friend to another".

What's on ya mind?

I'm sick & tired of these niggas out here in this world

Always tryna holla' & sex every girl

All they wanna' do is sex you & roll

On the other hand you wanna' give em your heart & soul

Interested in only laying on ya back

No time for commitment, just booty calls in fact

Whisper in ya ear, spittin' all that weak game

No nigga seems different, every man acts the same

But girls, we love that bad boy type

They ain't worth shit, can only lay pipe

There are some that love you and really care

The nice ones, a lil' corny, finish last, that ain't fair

Been lookin' so hard, where the good ones hiding at

All the decent ones, I love em, for ya'll I'll go to bat

So far & so few, one in a million, Aaliyah said it first

That last man I loved, got took away in a Hurst

The one before that, I loved him to death

He was my best friend, set apart from all the rest

Still wonder sometimes how his life is

If we were still together, we would've had more kids

But now I keep meeting these no good ass niggas

That got dough, but stingy and makin' six figures

Or the ones that be frontin', they really broke

Or think you sweet, and try to play you like a joke

Nowadays most niggas want a fat ass and cute face

I got news for ya'll; the next will take your place

I gotta' speak my mind, don't mean to be rude

I need a real man, someone special, not just any dude

True Love

Almost a life time and counting

But my feelings don't doubt me

Love compared to a brother

But close to none other

Yet a passion so real, can't help but to feel

Like it's truly meant to be

Love long, eternity

Distant mates of the soul

Lead by fear to play the role

Of a peer, an acquaintance

But been in love ever since

Now here lies the mystery

Too far apart, we cannot be

Broken hearts to make amends

Once in love but now just friends

Feelings surfaced, that walls kept hidden

For by love she is driven

Afraid of trust, scared of change

No regrets, in search of romance

Will it ever one day be

That you could ever love she?

Whose love runs deep for you

Now she can admit that this is true

As the weight lifts off her chest

A lil' ashamed, but none the less

Maybe a big mistake

Just couldn't live with the heartache

Want to keep the feelings hid inside

Until they crumbled up and died

But true love doesn't go away

These words tell what the heart won't say…

To all my Ladies:

Don't we all want a man to treat us right?

A man that's **faithful**, we can come home to each and every night

A man that's tough but at the same time so very sweet

Someone that's strong we really know we can't beat

He can be a thug and know how to put it down

And he must be real, we don't need a clown

He can be from the streets and can be a little hood

As long as he act right and treat a sistah good

It's ok if he got more than one kid

Don't mind if he was locked up and did a little bid

He can be a college man, of a business mind

Each one of us females attracts a different kind

Now down to the basics, we need a man who can dress

And keep up his appearance, not looking a mess

We love a smart man all dressed in a suit

And equally love a man rockin' that timberland boot

We need a man that doesn't nag and give us our space

At the same time ladies don't be all on his case

We all want a dude to spoil us rotten

Nobody that's sneaky always scheming or plotting

He gotta' be able to make us laugh and smile

We all want a relationship that's gonna' last for awhile

And guys don't forget we don't need the drama

That you got going on wit ya first baby momma

We all want a man that's tall dark and handsome

Someone that's special not just any bum

Oh, don't get me wrong light skinned dudes are in

We don't want a man that's slept wit' all of our kin

Girls all want men, confident, not conceited

To have a little dough, cause lord knows we need it

We all want a dude that has a good heart

If he ain't perfect, we'll still keep him, if we loved him
from the start

We need a man who understands us that always has our back

And if we lose our focus help us get back on track

We need him to support us in each and every way

Emotionally, physically, grow old wit us one day

Most important we want a man who cares for us in spite of

To give us all his attention and show us all his love.

Tell Me

Would you like me if I didn't have the cutest little face

Could you ever find a chic to fill my shoes or replace

Would you like me if my hair wasn't always tight

Or is the real reason you like me, 'cause we don't argue or fight

Would you like me if I wasn't so gangsta and hood

Would we be together if my attitude wasn't so good

Would you like me if I had a squad full of kids

Would you write or come visit if I did a few bids

Would you like me if I didn't spit all that fly game

Would you diss me if I was fat or would your love stay the same

Would you be my man if I was sick and had HIV

I don't blame you if you ran, 'cause it wouldn't be me

Would you like me if I didn't have a job or some dough

Would you wife me if you knew before you I was a hoe

Would you lie or keep it real if you cheated wit' another girl

Or would you think I'm stupid and say it was ya man Earl

Would you tell me if you liked guys and changed to being gay

Or would our relationship remain the same way

Would you buy me a fake diamond and say it was real

Would you like me if I couldn't cook or fix you a meal

Would you be wit' me if I cheated and had another man's seed

Would I be ya favorite girl if I couldn't roll up weed

Would you wife me if I was average and if I wasn't bad

Would you swallow ya pride & tell me I was the best girl you had

Would you like me if I didn't lace you and give you what you want

Would you love me or hate me if I wasn't so blunt

Would you tell me to my face or talk behind my back

If I had a nice body, but my personality was wack

Would you love me in spite of, 'cause I'm bound to make a mistake

Would you love me if I wasn't real, but I was frontin' or fake

These questions for all my niggas out there in the world

Do you love her or are you playin' ya girl?

Ready for Love

Wanna' flow positive and spit love songs

But I ain't feelin' dat' shit cause I keep getting wronged

By this one and that one, and just everyone I can think of

But that's how shit be goin' on in this so called life

Been from mistress, to wifey, to side jawn to jump off

Now I'm feelin' like they all need to step off

This dude that I'm feelin' claim he be busy

Know he got another bitch when he ain't fuckin' wit me

I don't know what he wants, but I'm his girl so he claims

But this dude got me sprung like the bull T-Pain

Now back to my love song and my poetry

Been lookin' for my mate but is he lookin' for me

Keep it real; speak my mind, no games, no frontin'

Just this bad ass bitch, chillin', smokin' and stuntin'

Gotta' crib, gotta' job, a lil' change on tuck

But no nigga by my side, down to ride, what the fuck?

Been thru it all even the hoeing around phase

But movin' on, cause honestly, been done wit' them days

Played wifey as a young jawn, had the kids and all

Lived the single life partyin' and havin' a ball

Had my dude dick me over had a baby on the side

Just stringin' me along on his lil' joy ride

Had a piece of heaven & hell on this so called earth

But Im'ma make it anyway been a survivor since birth

Been in fights wit' my dude wearin' black eyes & all

He thought I'd be by his side cause he played a lil' ball

NAW!!!

I wish love was perfect and trouble to cease

I spit game like any nigga that's why Im'ma beast

I need that "Unbreakable" love says Alicia Keys

You know the kinda' love that'll make you weak in the knees

Sittin' home by the phone each and every night

And if that nigga don't call, you be ready to fight

SIKE!!!

My nigga been locked up & I stood by his side

Sneakin' shit all in the jail 'cause he knew I would ride

Ridin' dirty in the whip up and down 95

Lucky I ain't booked for 20, for 10 or for 5

I need dat' B & Hova; Bonnie and Clyde type of shit

Ridin' down the E-way, gettin' head in the whip

I'm ready for love or whatever u call it

But dat' shit ain't come yet, so I continue to spit

Been from dat' ugly duckling, to this gorgeous swan

Done been stalked and harassed by this nigga named Twan

Caught a case wit' my man and we rode for each other

Then he whisper in my ear "Boo I love you like no other"

OK. This nigga did me wrong time and time again

Left me home wit the kids and a broken heart to mend

Yeah, him messin' wit dat' chick, matter fact my ex-friend

Feelings a lil' hurt, but you know that was back then

Oh! Don't get me wrong, it's no halo on my head

Done set niggas up for they change and they bread

A lil' grimey but loyal to the niggas I deal wit

Spoil 'em rotten, cook 'em meals, and all that good shit

I need love like LL said back in the day

All cuddled up in the winter, then break up around May

Ya'll know niggas ain't the only ones who get spring fever

Make you wifey when it's cold, then when it's hot leave her…

I went from this ghetto ass dime

To this thorough chick spittin' rhymes

So just listen real clear Im'ma tell you one more time

I'm ready to settle down & be all in love

Like the title of this poem "I'm ready for Love"

Why

It's been some years in countin' and we ain't even together

I done been there for you thru good and bad weather

I call you my friend but deep down inside

All this love I got for you I'm tryin' to hide it

I just wanna' know why?

You be treatin' me like this

Cause when somebody scoops me up

Who you really gone miss

You tell me I'm the best keep me always comin' thru

And since I can remember I only been dealin' wit you

You know that I love you, 'cause I'm always tellin' you

And if you don't got love for me then tell me who?

Been hidin' this so long, cause I don't wanna' lose you

But I gotta' tell you now if it's the last thing I do

You might as well call me yours, but you the only one who don't get it

And is all this waiting for nothing, or should I move on or just quit

You should really be mines but you cool wit how it is

No affection or commitment

Just a weekend handlin' biz

You should already know how I do, and how I roll

And I don't play no silly games my actions genuine, from the soul

Tired of these feelings, let's be honest, keep it real

Letting my guard down a lil' just to tell you how I feel

I think about you often but just don't let you know

And I be hurt sometimes, and don't let it show

I don't think I ever told you 'cause it was a hard time for me

But would things be better or worse if I would've kept that baby

I just wanna' know why

You don't love me how I love you

'Cause i'm the best girl you never had

When you gonna' get that clue

So what you waitin' on, what you wanna' find somebody better

You want me to be like them chicks only after some dough

You want me to be like her, always actin' all crazy

And I don't go for anything, gotta' be treated like a lady

Tryna be mad at you cause you not my man

But no one else could have me the way you can

No labels or titles, kinda like buddy

Really thinking to myself, does he really love me?

I just wanna' know why?

Am I the only one you care for? Or was that just a lie

Not just me huh? You got some other chick

Don't need no competition, need to be ya first pick

Back to the point, it's you and only you

And since you got this info, what you gonna' do

Not gonna' get my hopes up, ain't even gone try

Please tell me, I just wanna' know why?

I love you

So much time on my hands, so little to do

Sitting here I'm my room, singing love songs 'bout you

Hoping you're OK, always cross my mind

All the times we shared, if time could rewind

It's amazing how things happen, in the blink of an eye

And the weak always crumble while the strong get by

I want you to know, no one could ever take your place

You hold a spot in my heart that will never erase

Your smile, your style, everything about you, so sweet

It was meant to be, for us to even meet

I mean it when I say, I really miss you

And believe me when I tell you that *I love you…*

One & Only

So much alike, how could that be?

The way you act, the boy version of me

Could there be, another you in the world

Come to find out she's just a plain ole' girl

Both love the same movies and sing the same song

Can't stand being away from each other so long

Each so confident and so very smart

Hold special places in each other's heart

Still tryin' to figure out what you did to me

Too good to be true, it couldn't be

It may have been the smile or maybe your hair

Or was it the way you always used to stare

I know at first I didn't really care

Liked you back then, my feelings I didn't share

Care about you a lot, and I care how you feel

So are you my one and only

Is this really real?

Letters

You say you love me, I love you too

But when we're not together, what is it you do?

Rumors about, stirring up confusion

Open my eyes, to see what has been done

Is it true or not

Did **he** take my spot

Can't handle this, don't wanna' be involved

But sooner than later this must be solved

Lessons

Lesson number 1; never lie to your girl

Cause she got the power to mess up ya whole world

Lesson number 2, watch what you say

Cause you don't want the wrath that'll come your way

Lesson number 3; don't lie no matter what you do

Cause she trusted you, and hates to be lied to

What you do in the dark always comes to the light

And she seen it in ya eyes from that very first night

And if she take you back, and you do it again

You probably won't have a girlfriend

She Lies Too

You tell me one thing, and then do another

Just keep it real or don't even bother

Lie after lie is what you feed me

The truth already known, don't you see?

What happened to the trust?

What happened to the union?

One more time and I swear I'm done

What you scared of, why you gotta' lie

The rules written, you just gotta' abide

You would think it's the man, that's doin' the wrong

And you hurt me like this, after together this long

Its apart, not together that we should belong…

Hate Me

One to my left, the other on the right

Alone in the middle, should I run or fight

I say I'm no punk, so handle it, don't run

Pull out a blade, wish it was a gun

A lil' 22 or a 9 millimeter

Butterflies fill my stomach, but I know I can beat her

I'm not a fighter, I'm a lover

Temporarily undercover

But if I swing and miss

It's curtains I swear

I'm so alone, that's rare

Where are your friends when you need 'em

Just standin' here wit' this dumb look on my face

And she steady talkin'

Why did I have to be walkin'

I don't need this today

Calgon, please take me away

Time Will Tell

When the time is right
I'll be in your arms
Playing in your hair
Sittin' back watchin' Scarface
But only when the time is right

When the time is right
You'll be my only friend
What we share, so special
Can you imagine that
When and if the time is right

When the time is right
I'll be all yours
Our bond so strong
Our life complete
But only when the time is right

When the time is right
It'll be so perfect
Not even rushed
A never ending trust
Real recognize real,
But only time will tell

Best Friend...

Not sentimental, but somewhat funny

Always so serious, if I gotta' do wit' money

No matter all that we've been thru

You know I still love you

When it counts the most, you always got my back

Closer than a friend, like an over protective dad

The soul mate I never knew I had

My very best friend

Together 'til the end

The Boy Next Door

That one special boy, what can I say about you

First I wish you success in everything you do

So handsome, intelligent, and talented too

Been ready for the next, just waitin' on you

You know what they say outta' mind, outta' sight

Alone in the corner, sittin', thinkin' and writin'

Always makin' jokes, always make me laugh

Appreciate you much, like a hot bath

All that we've been thru; still love you with a smile

That boy next door, we gonna' be friends for awhile

FAMILY

Little Cousin

Believe in yourself, you are very smart

Always hold a place in your loved ones heart

Life is full of surprises and fun

Live life to the fullest, you only get one

Don't front for no one, always keep it real

Never be afraid to tell people how you feel

Stays focused in the streets, and keep your cool

Trust me when I say, those niggas can wait

And there'll always be some girls that do nothing but hate

Do your best, keep ya head held high

Because you won't succeed if you don't try

Mother

This poem goes out to my one and only mother

With everything we been thru, indeed I do love her

Dear mom, this next verse, I wanted to say

Your very special to me, you came a long way

Let me tell you exactly how I feel

No lies, no games, just keepin' it real

Over the past few years I've developed as a poet

Without being in jail you wouldn't even know it

My heart goes out to you everyday

And though I may not call, it remains to say

I love you as much as can be

And I know in your heart that you love me.

Dear Bra'

For years, the only brother I had

Just me, you and my dad

Were always so close and tight

Didn't really argue and fight

The years flew by and we grew apart

It's gotta' be time for a new start

So many stories to share, so much time passed by

The words very few, sometimes I could cry

Still my ace boon coon, my favorite little brother

All those times I turned to you, instead of our mother

Sometimes I miss you, but still stay strong

And my heart still cries from that Aaliyah song

I wish we could go back, all the good times we had

And when I look back on life, it wasn't so bad

Reminisce

Reminiscing of old times & how things used to be

Back in the day grew up in the center, just my brother and me

Some days good & some bad, we always had each other

My best friend in the world, known as my little brother

Ridiculed for wearing glasses, elementary school

Used to hurt back then, but now it's all cool

Now, emerged into beautiful butterflies

Didn't have a lot, but still managed to get by

Down in Maryland, Chillum road, across the block from D.C.

When grand mom and Mr. Jerry used to bring us grocery

All the memories on Pine road, that black dog, Jake

Up at 803, grand mom Helen, baking a cake

I'll never forget the parties, New Year's night

On grand pop George's birthday, all in the world seemed right

I remember 438, even though I was young then

Used to pee in the bed and blame Lauren

On Main street in Darby, where I had that first kiss

Looking back, it's times like those I miss

What about Morton, 15 Main Street

No family or friends, people I didn't wanna meet

Remembering when my dad 1st met Ms. Geraldine

Didn't like her back then, too proud, too mean

It took some time, but had to get to know her

Now I can say I love her like a mother

Ms. Nadine what can I say, you were by my side

One of the best grand moms we have, everything aside

Val, I first met you, summer '98

Drove ya cousins blue blazer on our first date

I can go on & on reminiscing of old times

Writing 'em down on paper, makin' little rhymes

So many memories, so many stories to share

Sittin' back wonderin' why life ain't always fair

So to all my people's that passed away thru time

To all of ya'll I dedicate, Reminisce, this heartfelt rhyme.

ACKNOWLEDGMENTS

"Trust in the Lord with all your heart, lean not to your own understanding, in all your ways acknowledge him and he will direct your paths. Proverbs 3:5-6"

To my children, NaTaijah, Asiah & Avon, you kids are the best thing that ever happened to me. I love you all to death. Tay; never be scared to be who you are, be genuine in everything you do. I appreciate you more than you will ever know. You have grown into such a beautiful young lady, the world better watch out!, you're the next great business woman of the world. Asiah; and I would never be able to make it without you. You helped me grow up, you will always be my baby! Never lose yourself, no matter what people may say or do. You are definitely a special person. You showed me how to love when I forgot how to. Avon, my one and only baby boy, truly a blessing, you brought me to my senses, back to reality. You came at the right time and place in my life. Keishana, I love you like a daughter, I want you to be the best mother and woman you can be. Never sell yourself short, you are worth so much more than you realize! God doesn't set you up for failure. Be true to yourself, and take care of your girls. And I will always have your back, no matter what! Jabe, you've given me a glimpse into the future of helping to raise a young man, I love you like you were my very own son. Dad, what can I say, I love you to death! You are my hero! You were the best father a girl could ask for and more. Mom, Wow! I love you to pieces, I hope when I'm your age I look as good as you. But seriously, you're more than a mother to me, you're like my best friend. Willi Million$, you were my best friend for a long time, I loved growing up with you, from Twp. to Atl. (lol), chameleons huh...I can't wait to cash that check you gave me. I'm not gonna turn this into a ghetto shout out section, so to my family, friends and anyone who has ever had my back or been by my side, you all have my love. Last but not least, T. Benson Glover, you definitely helped me become a stronger person. From those long talks to your mini sermons and all that fell in between, thank you. I appreciate you much more than I could ever show, you will always have my love. To anyone I have ever hurt or wronged in my lifetime, I sincerely apologize, please forgive me. It's so funny, I started writing poetry just to vent because I kept my feelings to myself, and I never thought it would be more than just my own personal collection. It has helped me to express thoughts that were suppressed in me for what seems like forever. As I share my gift, I pray it reaches hands and hearts as inspiration and motivation, that you can do anything through Christ who strengthens you.

Piece of Mine

By LaTrese D McCullough